singing

my mother

down

Elyria Rose

Emerald Tablet Designs ❖ Medina, OH

ISBN 978-1539051152
ISBN 1539051153

Design and photography by Elyria Rose

For you, Mom.

and for Mohonk —

where so many memories were
made before & after my mom's diagnosis.
May your memories in this place
be more of gladness, less of sorrow!

♡ Delphine

Contents

Foreword

A few months after my mother died, I changed my name to Elyria. It was a rite of passage suggested by a dear friend who had lost a parent some years earlier.

My mother was diagnosed with multiple myeloma in 2007. It's a relatively rare form of cancer that attacks bone marrow, and at the time there was no reliable cure. I was visiting her when the disease first flared up and sent her to the hospital. I ended up taking care of her for part of that summer, after she got out of the hospital and came home with multiple hairline fractures in her spine.

It was a hard summer. I got married at the end of it, though, and she was well enough to dance at the wedding. That goal was one of the ways she got through the days when the pain was so bad it took her an hour of solid effort to get up off the couch. She wasn't strong enough to walk upstairs to her bed.

She rallied. Symptoms got worse. Things went back and forth for years. She hated the idea of losing her hair, was determined to avoid the kinds of chemo that would make it fall out. She took charge of her care, and her doctor was incredibly supportive. Her health insurance covered nearly everything. So many things went right. So many people supported her – and they supported me, too, when I was in town looking after her.

In late 2012 she asked me to come back to Massachusetts again, take care of her again for a month or so while she went through a harder round of chemo. I took a leave of absence from work, and went. It was hard on my husband, hard on our marriage, and hard on me, but if I could do things over I wouldn't change anything about that decision. In the end, I stayed for six months, not one. I left the job. I took care of her as well as I could, and when I couldn't do a good job any more, I helped her find home health aides to fill in for me. I tried to visit every month, after that. I didn't talk about how hard it was to watch her health failing, or how grief always walked with me.

I always knew, without thinking about it head on, that one day the cancer would claim my mother's life. We tried to live around that knowledge, she and I, and most of the time we did a pretty good job. I tried not to tell her how scared I was of losing her. She held me when it came out anyway.

I learned so many things from her. She was a brilliant scientist, a professor of astronomy, and a deeply spiritual person. She built a stone circle – the UMass. Sunwheel – that still stands on the Amherst campus today, to educate the public about our place in the universe. But more than that, I learned how to love and how to be kind from her. I learned how to be curious, and stubborn, and stick to my guns no matter what other people said. And I learned what it feels like to be loved, more than any other person in someone's world.

I never learned how to live without her until after she was gone.

The poems in this book are how I learned it. How I'm still learning it. I still miss her, and I still wish she were here, and I still hate the cancer that destroyed her body. I still love her. Living without her doesn't mean ignoring those feelings; it only means that the feelings don't consume me. It means that I get to live my own life. Part of doing that, for me, is recognizing and honoring the ways I'm still connected to my mother.

I wish she could read these words. I know some of them would have made her cry, and sometimes that would have been what she needed.

More than that, I want you to read these words. I know some of them will make you cry, and sometimes that will be what you need. I want you to read them, and remember how to heal, learn to live with the hurts and the losses you carry – take a deep breath – and go on living. With time, and care, you can be whole again.

We are all alone in our grief, sometimes. But other times, we can find comfort in sharing our sorrows with others who have lived through loss. We come away stronger for it.

That is my hope for you.

all my love,
Elyria

singing
my mother
down

I. Grief

on the occasion of my mother's death

There is a hole near the center of this web I call my life
So near that sometimes I cannot see it
and before I think, I want to tell you
About the raven feather I found on a hike.

And I cannot. You are no longer contained
in a body with a phone that has a number I can call.
So you know what you and the rest –
the rest is up to me now.

But to fill this hole where you were will take years.
It will take a life well lived and a thousand thousand
        memories of you,
in joy and sorrow and wind and firelight.

It will take more courage than I have.

It will take each of you here, today,
telling the people you love just how much you love them.
It will take your gardens blooming with all the colors of
        the rainbow.
It will take unthinkable acts of kindness
in the moments you least expect them,
        to strangers, and family, and friends.

It will take all the breath in my body
and all the words in my mouth
and it will take sharing them with you.

Or perhaps there is no gap, no empty place, no hole...
perhaps you have simply stepped aside
and now I see the world itself was always standing
        with you.

In that case, the smallest flower and the brightest star
would each remind me of you
even as they made me smile
        with joy that wells up at the sheer improbability
that a flower or a star should exist, let alone
that I should exist to see them.

And I begin to understand that both are true.
There is a hole; there is not a hole.
You are here; you are not.
Maybe quantum physics isn't so impossible to
        understand
if I can understand that.

For as long as I live, I will miss you.
For as long as I live, thinking of you will make me smile,
and, sometimes, ask myself the questions
I need to ask, the kind
that always came to mind when I saw the amazing,
deliberate way you chose to live.

        Are you happy?
        Did you remember to hug the people you love today?
        Have you drunk enough water?
        Can you be the person you want to spend the rest
            of your life with?
        What are your dreams?
        Will you remember to laugh and sing and love,
            and to just be?

To those questions, my only answer is
that I will keep asking them,
of myself and of the people I love.
And I will remember how beautiful you were in asking,
and that your answers touched the sky.

know me

I think you only asked my name,
but I heard your real question.
Who am I?

It used to be
that my mother knew the answer.
Now that she is gone,
I try to hold it for myself,
but it is hard. Each time
I assert that yes -
this thought, this act, shows
exactly who I am -
the eyes of death
meet mine.

So the answer, the real answer,
is only that I am.
I sleep, sometimes I dream.
I wake up and get out of bed.
I eat. Work. Exercise. Write.
These things are not the measure
of who I am, but they are building blocks,
a place to stand.

On bad days
when I cannot do the things I think I should
my lover reminds me
that I am still grieving
and holds me.

On good days I can look ahead and understand
that I will always be becoming who I am.
On good days, grief is a part of me
that I can learn to carry.

But I am wise enough to know
that I will need you to know me,
to restore me to myself
on the bad days, when the most that I can do
is so much less
than all I lost
the day my mother died.

integral

When the female-bodied person awakes
                from the enveloping sadness
                                she does not recognize her life

                                        She sits in a room
                                with a book, a can of paint
                with days that pass in ways she no longer
                        understands

        she thinks in images when words refuse to come
                                                all that is
                                        left, she realizes
                                                        is
                                        self
                        the rest has been stripped away
                nothing remains but what is integral
                and she is her sole remaining calculus

        she craves simplicity, she lives it
                        even as it stifles her.
        perfect enlightenment, chiseled despair
                hang from the ceiling, drape the walls
                        The only things that still have meaning
        are those that mar the balance in this room,
                        waiting for a hand to set them right

but she cannot stand to move them.
        Would it not empty out the very sea of meaning
and make her children
                        (she laughs bitterly - she has none)
                as bleak as she has been?

        what was it that woke her in this room, geometric,
                        integral?
                is there something here she needs to do?

these are the things
she has forgotten how
to know.

so she looks to you, beautiful and hollow-eyed.

What would you say to her,
this female-bodied shape
within your mirror
who has forgotten how to live?

she never lost her hair

in the dream
my mother is upset.
she is losing her hair.
she brushes it but long hanks
come off and stick in her brush.
she puts on a bright bandanna.

i can fly, and i can carry her, so
together we soar over the bridge, over water,
to a sheltered vale in the mountains.
we grin at each other. we laugh
at how limitless we are.

she is tiny. she is frail,
but i feel her strength.

have we come full circle, now?
now my turn is here.
i cradle her, too dear for words,
we feel no fear
of falling or of death.

death has already visited us,
and still we find time
to fly, in my dreams.

i read her journals.

my life
still twines with hers,
with the long strands of her silver hair
that hide, mischievous,
in a sheltered vale in the mountains, and
beneath my pillow.

to madness

With enlightenment, death!
               the gull cries
            nameless, mocks the warranty of souls
         all is ended, save
                  one taunting gleam of chance,

      mirage, maybe, that lingers wrapped in
               fog while demented revelers dance.

      No structure on this path can be foretold
            no foresight to untangle silk
      to prophecy, tapestry, show what still might be
      no hand to soothe the wounds that never heal.

Know you what these words all mean?
               I do not. I set them down to set them free,
         and that alone
                  sets me apart from most who speak.

      Or perhaps it sets them all apart from me,
               lying twixt their glib and pointed teeth,
         pretending insight, when they cannot see.

                  The serpent would I court, the tongue
         that forks yet pierces with the lightest
                  scrape of truth across unscaly skin.
Attack me, serpent!
                     Take me whole!
         Constrict my body, if you cannot find my soul!

            Recoil then, recoil.
                  Leave me be!
         If not for dinner, not for life, you
                  shall have no part of me.

22

Dreaming back again to do no more than dream
        I slip with measured grace

                I flee the haunted laughs of
        those who've seen
      the nature of this place.

My path beneath the twisted tree
        must pass, chill and serpent-fell;
          this grief is far too deep for me
      and I must follow it to madness,
        or beyond,
              where none can tell.

maybe a graph would help

when those things that are not needed fall aside

simplicity pulls my soul

into a spiral dance so fierce

I have to look away.

These are only moments, movements.

To sustain this angle

would be to approach my own death

and laugh.

Movement by moment, chance by choice,

asymptotically, perhaps,

we sidle closer to that elusive point where

will and wisdom fuse.

From there, I wonder

what would remain of life,

but to slide on down the spiral

to the stars?

sometimes grief still strangles me

I am sorry.

I cannot speak today.

the birch

it must be peaceful
to be a tree

      wind

          light

              water

seasons pass and you
simply are

no need to rush, no need
to worry

no need to know
what you need

for if you need and do not receive
you die

and if you receive, then
you blossom when the season is right.

and yes, a time will come
when your skin breaks
and that which is you
departs
and your trunk falls
to rejoin the soil

but for a time, those who see you
will have said
what a beautiful tree

and you, lovely birch,
you will not have worried
what that means.

quiet

I feel
as if I have been asleep
for many hundred years. Within, there
wells a quiet so deep
I am almost frightened.
If I were wise,
I would be terrified of that silence.
But I am not.

So, sometimes, when I'm alone
I let the quiet take me.

I exert no pressure

on the world.

I

am.

In that place,
there is no need
to do more.
But my respite there is never long.

Probably, that is a good thing.
If I stayed, I would forget who I am,
or remember it. I do not know
what that would do to me.

Such a noisy thing, to ask,
who am I?
The question grows an answer.

I am more
than the sum of what I have done. I -

I am a creature of thought, and nebulae,
of wild places and of rhymes.
And more. I am
what you believe me to be. So
tell me who you think I am,
if you can see beyond
this welling quiet.

unthinkable

My eyes snap open to blackness.

I clutch after more of the dream, try to fill in
blank places where there is a feeling story should be.

The water has gone down enough now
that we can leave camp. Before we do,
I move around the grounds and
through the house, check
that no one has forgotten anything.
The young boy who lives in the house stares
at a tapestry. When I go into his room, the bedding
hangs to the floor, makes
a cave of the space beneath his bed.
I lift to check for things forgotten.
He cries out and flings himself around
to the other side of the bed,
gives himself to the white dog we all thought
had died when it vanished, years ago,
the curly-haired, impeccably trained dog to which he fed
his parents, and now feeds
himself.

The rest of the night, ghosts
of the boy and his hungry dog haunt me.
How could we have known?
The same island returns, waters receded fully now.
The driveway is passable.
People avoid the house, move
around it, eyes averted against
the impossible shame of that proud place.

So it is in the waking world also.
The unthinkable happens.
Our imaginations never compass what went wrong
until it is too late.

We do not wake up.

the lake

it's my secret place. I would
show it to you if I could, but you
wouldn't see it if I did.

At best you'd see its shadow,
    dark beneath my eyes.
At worst you'd see a brittle smile
    and think that it was bright.

I've dealt with it so well. Always together,
    on top of things, friendly, the details managed.
You tell me you care.
How can I tell you that the only thing I feel
    is my mother's absence?

I need to scream before I say another word.

I don't. I bury it.
        Another day, another phone call,
            and, yes. I'm grateful for what she left me, and,
                yes. I care about you too.

But I have drowned my heart
        so you wouldn't see me cry. I have hidden my grief
            and the tears I still hold back
                to fill this secret place.

        Dark water, darker sky,
    and the water's always rising.
Everywhere I go, I keep it by me,
    to my left and one step back.

If you feel a cool wind when I walk by,
or a little touch of sorrow,
it's as close as I can get you
to my dark and secret place.

contagion

Houses can be terribly empty. I should know;
I organize them for a living.
And I love what I do. I sing
the space to order from each bewildering
sameness of chaos. The work
is absorbing, an end
in itself. Fulfilling. But

I have noticed, often enough, a feeling
that creeps around corners,
corners where the dust has been
tidied away. A seeping, creeping
emptiness, even in the houses
where vibrant people live. It
does not feel like ghosts, not hungry,
just hollow. A hollowness

of form, as if every thing I touch
in these houses is no more
than clay slapped sloppily around
some imagined weight. The weight shifts
when I am there. It forgets why
it was once important, and I
can say, without missing it,

goodbye. And I mention this only because
the emptiness creeps from houses
into me, sometimes.
I forget why
I was once important, and I
say, without feeling it,
goodbye.

Invisible

My grandfather refuses to call me by my name.
I changed it recently, you see, in the wake
of loss. And to me,
that new name is who I am,
who I am becoming.

But he cannot or will not let go
of who he thinks I am, who
he wants me to be. Perhaps
he wants me to sit
in some box he made that never fit me.
Or he does not believe such a simple change
could mean so much to me.
The name is, after all, only a few letters different.

My grandmother apologizes for him, and tries
earnestly, I think, to remember my new name.
She forgets, but each time, I find
I can smile, and before I correct her, I
have already forgiven her. She
has not realized
that what my grandfather will not do
she cannot make up for.

When I try to stand where he does, see
myself from his perspective,
all is firm, unyielding, brittle. He must
see all the world this way. Has he forgotten
that once he was young, that he grew?
Does he separate everything he sees
from older versions of itself, so that he
can blinker out change as it happens
all around him, all the time?

I do not know, and soon, I tire of
trying to put my mind where I imagine his must live.
I would rather be myself, my real self,
the self named by my real name, the one

that points to me.

If he will not do it, he cannot see me. That
is the choice he makes every time
he refuses to call me by my name.

Do not think me cruel, if I visit less often.

I do not want to be invisible.

the curve

there is an unavoidable, peculiar familiarity
to this one curve that I cannot escape,
something between the curve of a bent head
and the graceful arc of a branch

not docility, not submission
but the way my mother's head
leaned tired into the pillow
on the hospital bed where she died

my wrist, as I held this notebook
displayed that same curve,
the same -- is it resignation?
acceptance? surrender
to our ultimate end?

maybe it's plain tiredness.
recognition that it's hard to hold your head up, finally,
when you've had cancer for nine years
lost forty percent of your body weight
and six inches in height,
hard to hold a notebook
when you're crying.

people laugh and talk around me,
and I curl, tired,
lean my head against a cushion,
rest on the solidity of one thing I know to be true.

I miss my mother desperately
even though I'm relieved her suffering is over.

When I am not afraid I'll end like her --
that this curve of the neck we share
means I too will succumb to death --
I take comfort in the way
the world keeps some of those things that were hers

so that I see them, in myself,
in the imagined curl of the young dragon's neck just
after it hatches.

I take comfort that the way
my head rests on this pillow
does not mean breath is ending,
but gives me strength
to raise my head again, soon,
and go on.

honey in the rain

Life had been grey for some time. Details
matter less than those fleeting impressions
that somehow remain. Endless
misting rain, never enough
to be a storm, never clearing.

Hands on a keyboard, stilled for just a moment, the
strong but untraceable impression
that they are wrist up,
though she could see her fingers resting on the keys.

No knowing what that meant, but
the sensation odd enough to stand out.
That was how life felt.

So imagine her surprise, imagine
how everything changed
when your smile sparked an answering smile
from her. Imagine that it was not
the clouds clearing, nothing
that sudden or bold or revelatory, no,
but there was a drop, a solid drop
of honey, that fell with the rain.

She happened to stand under it, head back,
mouth open, as it fell, and
landed, impossibly sweet, on her tongue.

The fresh smell of the earth in spring, suddenly
sweetened, suddenly
more than it had been. And she
stared up into the sky, unbelieving,
not understanding how sweetness can come
from anywhere, from those greying rainclouds that
refuse
to let sunlight through.

Sometimes, now, when she sits silent
in front of a keyboard of her own,
a smile walks across her face.
Slow. It moves, languid, that smile,
and any who knew her

would know that it moved at the exact speed
of a single drop of honey
falling with the rain.

Leonids

Driving home. It's the night
of the Leonids, early August,
warm wind. I lean forward, look up

and stars flash over the dashboard.
Music loud, windows down,
I fly along the highway

swift as the falling stars.
The only thing missing in this moment
is you.

Apology

I am so sorry. All those years,
all that pain,
and what I was really seeking
was a feeling
that, around you,
I did not feel.

It wasn't lack of love. I loved you
with as much of me
as I thought you could accept, as much
of me as I knew
to offer.

But time and sorrow pushed me down to feelings
that run deeper than love,
bedrock to the soul.
I have no name for them.
I only know
that they are tied
to fierce and wild, ancient things.

And still the discovery goes on,
secretive thing that I am,
all mirrors and flashes of insight
and slippery shifting kernels
that are true
but are not bedrock.
The ancient and the fierce,
they anchor me
so I'm not blinded by those flashes
so my inner vision clears.

You were my love
when both of us were young.
And I am so very sorry
that I was less gentle with you
than I could have been.

If I could go back, return
in time with what I have found
I would have taken you with me to the desert,
to the ruins of other worlds
and I would have told you simply
that if you decided to stay
it would change our lives.
I hope, if I had known to say it,
that you would have joined me
and found a spot beside me near those fierce and
ancient things,
in the desert, let our fingers tangle
in the dust.

I am sorry
I found no name
for what I needed.
And I am sorry you remained behind.

I cannot be sorry
for needing what I need –
strange as it may seem –
though I wish I could have said all this
when it still mattered.

I need fierce, ancient things; for that,
no apology except to admit, finally,
that in their searing intensity
the mirrors of my soul
catch fire. And near them,
I am all of me;
near the bedrock, with
these ancient things
I am aflame.

living with death

There was a time
of silence. I would not look
at what was coming. I feared
death's shadow as it crept
around the yard. I let fear suck
life and words from me,
before death came to stay.

Now, death lives with me
and in its shadow
I understand that words
are worth little, unshared.

There is nothing morbid in living
with death. Living without it,
that was when
I was unable to speak.
Living without death, I
only lived a half-life, afraid
of things I did not want to name.
Now that fear is gone.

Now, I am not afraid of death.
And I want you
to be more afraid of
a life half-lived
than you are
of life's inevitable
end.

II. Love

jewels / sunday morning 1

this morning
when the light began
I opened my eyes

you were there, nearer than belief
I lay still so I would not disturb you as you slept

I tried to slip back into sleep, breathed with you

but somewhere between sleeping and awake
I lost the desire to be anywhere
other than exactly where I was

my eyes filled with tenderness
if you had woken up to see me crying
I would have said

don't worry, this isn't sadness
this is mortality,
recognition that moments like this do not come so often

this is my heart, too full to do anything
but shed these jewels into a pillow
and watch you sleep

but my tears were silent
and I moved through the moments when they burned
out from my eyes.

I held you as you slept,
as the light grew stronger
as I wept.

something beautiful

I want to make something beautiful. I want to make
something you would love to read. You'd turn the pages
over and over, and when you got to the end you'd go
right back to the beginning. You wouldn't want to stop
looking at it. But I would build in points to help you
pause and look away. We couldn't have you neglecting
the rest of your life just to look at it, even if it was the
most beautiful thing in the world. Beauty is in the eye of
the beholder, they say, and your eyes were the loveliest
I've ever seen. So you might have thought it was more
beautiful than you. The mirrors always led you astray.
But I didn't.

I suppose I did make something beautiful. With you. We
were close. Very close, in the end. You carried me into
the world, I carried you out of it. I miss you. I want to
make this beautiful thing so I can show people the way
you looked at the world. The way you looked to the
stars, and never tired of looking. that you loved each
blossom in your garden, every stem and stone. I want
other people to see beauty the way you saw it.

Things that are beautiful usually don't last. I want this
to be forever. I want the balance, the lightness, of all the
sunrises and sunsets we ever watched over the low hills
of home. I want the flight of the redwing blackbird,
forever. I want to make something you would love with
all your wide and open heart. I want to make something
beautiful. It's the only way I can show you how much i
love you. It won't bring you back, I know that, but it can
carry your heart forward and plant it in people, rare
people, and they will feel themselves uncurl, unfurl
when they read this thing I want to make. They will
open like you. They will not be you. I will not fool myself
there. I guess I can live with that.

It would be better, living would, if I knew how to make
something this beautiful. I want it to inspire tenderness.

I want it to ease the hearts of everyone who reads it. I want it to change the world, to make of this broken place a place that is learning how to heal. I want to do for everyone what I could not do for you. I want to take beauty and mold it in my hands to make a thing that heals. I could share it out, then, hand a little bit of it to everyone I meet. I would have to go out more into the world then, so I could meet more people and share more of that thing. I would do it, even on days when I'd rather stay home. I would do it for you.

I want to make something beautiful because the world is less beautiful without you in it. I want to make something beautiful to fill this empty place in me. I even try to be something beautiful, to give the credit for making it to you. It doesn't matter who makes it, I suppose, you, me, or a million people. Most of all, I want it to be beautiful. I want people to turn to it for comfort on hard days. I want it to fortify the grieving ones, to help them breathe and walk and feel their lives again. I want to jolt the ones who do harm, stop them in their tracks, open a door for them to walk through, open them to change.

I want to make something beautiful. I want to dedicate it to you, when I do. I want to read it to you. I want to be able to pause and laugh or cry with you whenever we need to. I would love to do that with you. If you were only here, I would. As it is, I will have to be content with wanting, until the time comes when I can make something beautiful. Until that day, know that this seed is growing in me. And though you'll never see it, this much is always true:

I want to make something beautiful
for you.

clamor

Too much
clamors in the world
too much cries look! look
at me at this, buy one get another, you
know you need me to be happy!
You know you do!

No. What I need
is a quieter world, where
I can hear birds sing at dusk and dawn.
Where the passing trains
only shake through once, twice a day, where
people want no more
than they need
and know it, when they don't need
more than they have.

So I have nothing to say to the clamoring throng.
They could not hear me if I screamed.
And I like talking better
when I can do it quietly, with you,
where you can hear me.

To you, I would say this.
When you walk in the wider world
as all of us must at times
please, as a favor to me,
don't stay longer than you have to.
I worry, you know,
about your hearing. Can
the cilia of the inner being
stiffen with exposure
as the cilia of your ears do?

And what will you miss
if all you are able to hear
is the clamor

of those who want more,
and more, and more?

I would trade all that forlorn cacophony
for one single coo
of a mourning dove, for the way
it fades to silence.

Himalaya

I live whole lives
in the gaps between your words.
Your pauses swell with possibility, with meaning
implicit, imagined, fine,
and flawed.

Flawed, I say,
because in them your desire plays no part.
Mindscapes, mine-scapes, crafted by absence and desire
are no substitute for the unimaginable richness
that is sharing lives.

Lives shared are never perfect,
but they are real, imperfect, and compelling as the traps
that riddle the Himalaya.

Let us climb, stumble at the lips of those yawning
crevasses, scale
those impossible heights, let us
meet the vast valleys and vaster sky.
Let us know each other.

If we do not, the gaps
between our words, selves,
will be forever laden with possibility so immense
we will never know how the sky
opens, how the mountains hold their
breath, when we dare
to speak.

winter song

walking out to the coffeeshop down the street
a cool windless afternoon following the freeze

a short woman in a long black coat walks towards us,
white head bowed
she looks up

and we had never expected to stop and meet a stranger
let alone one who would point so true at everything
we had been thinking of but never quite saying

she stopped, she said, because I was beautiful
she stopped because she was lonely and recognized
something in us
that she needed to speak to
and we needed to hear

it was when she sang and her voice reverberated
through the streets that I first
understood, here is someone
someone I've never met but already care for, and

if she can walk down the street and meet two young
strangers and enthrall them
then her stories are worth hearing
and so are mine.

she asked us our heritage. are we Scottish? yes, we said,
and no, for we are
many things
she worked at university, she said, because they heard
her singing.
she has a black belt in karate and
when she worked with the FBI after the war, hunting
Nazis
they chose her because if things got dangerous she
she could take care of herself

what languages do we speak?
not as many as she, who has lived in sixteen countries
and learned the tongues of nine.
not Russian?
Russian, you need your mother tongue, she said, or you
will be lost.

I paint. do you see my nails? from oil paint and
turpentine.
I will show you my paintings.
a small green case holds faded photographs of beautiful
women she had captured
but the light had seeped into them and they need a lot
of work now.
her scarf was white and grey velvet, and she was cold.

how old am I, she said
I saw her hair and how she looks like my grandmother
did a few years ago
84, I guessed, and 60, said he
she didn't hear and made us guess again. then told us
she is 87.

one day she looked down and there was a green spot
crawling on her foot.
she adopted the lizard.
she had a boa too, but she had to give him up. they
need exercise and
she did not have enough space for him to crawl in, he
was sloppy
and she loved him.

she was a teenager during world war II and she lived
in the forest, taught the two others with her
to climb the trees, and she motioned
as if climbing with a belt, to swing
from tree to tree, to eat worms, and bugs, and snakes,
to chew the meat off the bone or wherever it was.
we survived a year and 7 months
until the war ended. May 21, 1945. then she studied.

she is old, she said, old,
and this thing she does now, it is not singing!
she has two PhDs and a black belt in karate. She knows
how to stay loose when she falls. She just did.

she was visiting her daughter in rehab
her cats, the shy one and the fierce one, are her family
now
her husband is dead.
when he was dying he said to her, I am forgetting
everything, I am going nuts up here.
No! she said, it is not you. The world is nuts, not you.
Not you.

she sings to us, operatic,
her voice rich and unexpected. I don't know the songs
until she get to
hava nagila, and I take her arm
we dance a single turn and she hugs me.

she smiles when he sings to her, for his voice is rich too,
and unexpected.
and all I can think is, I am glad I know that dance.
he reminds me to give her my card,
and she says she will call me. she sings again.
we hug.

she cries, shoos us on our way to the coffeeshop, kisses
my hand
and I will not let this moment fade.
it is this, the connection of self to other selves, that
binds our world together,
lets us live through the unfairness, the squalor, the
hate, the terrible absence of feeling
and still find moments of joy
in chance meetings on the street in winter. Even though
she will never call,
I will not forget her songs.

condensed

poetry condenses
this business of living

call / response
balance / falling

this path we walk
is calling

the things you want
are all I need

hands are shaking
desire awaking, freed

in that dance I always dance
with the desert, centered, home
you are more than welcome

so if I skew the balance
in secret greed

be blunt
I will be forgiving

falling / walking
taking / giving

when I am with you
meaning condenses

I want the poetry
of living

hello again, soul

It's been a long time since we talked.
This may sound cruel, and I'm sorry, but we did agree to
be honest with each other;
you're not looking so hot.

Tired, are you? Or tarnished? It's hard to understand
you sometimes.
Lonely? Is that it? Ah, that resonates. Lonely.
I've been lonely, every so often. No, not often. Have I? I'm
not sure I'm remembering this right.

Who do you wish was here now? Someone to hold you,
someone to talk with?
Maybe you don't miss a person at all.
You do that sometimes, soul... I do remember.

You miss places.
You shut it up so easily, it makes me forget how
attached you are.
I'm sorry we can't go there. We have a life, you know.

You want the desert - mountains - harsh lands -
places that mirror who you know we are.
You want us to walk for hours, the way we used to -
before life got so complicated and full.
Of course I remember! How could you think.... all those
beautiful talks we had...
Oh, my heart, I am so sorry.

Why don't you tell me these things?
Is it that you don't want to make me unhappy? please,
I would rather be unhappy than let you hide the truth
from both of us.

Well. What do you need me to do?

If you need me to leave, I'll do as much as I can. I can't
promise we'll go.

But please, tell me what you need, always!
I can't bear you like this, small and curled up and half-
invisible, even to me. I'm so sorry.
And I do promise that whatever else happens, we'll talk
more than we have for a long time. Maybe we should
stay up all night together again. It should be sometime
soon, before you stop trusting me, and before you get so
small I forget you're here.

I wish I'd known before how unhappy you are.
I suppose all I had to do was ask - maybe I was afraid
to.
I probably was. I'm not that brave, really.
Let's talk tonight, while we're sleeping. Tell me a story,
and in the morning I'll tell it back to you.

That's a good place to begin.
Give me your hand - we'll shake on it -
we'll see what kind of story you've been dreaming up.

Maybe it's a story from the desert. I hope it is.
You too? Good.
That's very good.
Good night.

Shadows

I. I am driving along the highway from
Flagstaff to Albuquerque.
Moonlight floods the land. My eye
snags on junipers that hunch
by the side of the road.

Shadows crouch behind each squat tree,
sharp enough that even my
headlight-blinded eyes
can pick them out at 80.

I'm going to miss these bright night-sky shadows.

II. Long ago, before I knew you were real,
I heard echoes of your pain.
Songs. Stories.
That unfailing rhythm in the background,
like wheels across pavement,
someone doing what was needed. But the rules
changed, and everything you did
means now that you are wrong.
You are the problem, you -
loyal, unflinching, bound -
your hurt and yes, your death, will never
convince you
to forgive yourself.

And I have felt your echoes all my life. I would like
to say to you, I do not understand
this world, but I honor you.
I do not forgive you
because you do not need forgiveness from me.

One day, perhaps, we will meet, and I will tell you
about shadows.

III. The shadows behind the juniper
take on a life of their own.
They do not move, they
do nothing you would not expect
of the shadow of a desert scrub in moonlight.

But I feel them watching me, keen
and prickly, even
through the windows of the car.

They see me as I fly past, but
I have 30 hours still to go
before I hit Ohio. And if I stayed to walk
with you, you there behind the juniper,
would I forfeit a night sky
I've never known?

IV. I wish I knew what shadows see. They show us
ourselves, but I don't know if they cast us
onward to the sky or into
some inner, deeper dark.

Clear beneath the desert moon, they
remain, and I am going 80, and
I cannot bear to leave them.

Bright shadows trace their way down my cheeks,
arroyos in the moonlight. The juniper
may never forgive me if I leave.
And I may never forgive myself
if I stay.

the light / sunday morning 2

this morning
the light woke me early
and found you in my arms.

the light was faint, but you were solid
and somehow so was I.

I lay awake and marveled for a while,
unmoving, breathing light.

I had not dared to dream
that the memory of a moment like this
would be mine.

your skin was warm against mine
and the planes of your face in the early light
hummed with presence.

I let my eyes drift closed, content,
but the memory was not complete,
and I could not bear to be anywhere
but here with you.

when I opened my eyes once more they were full
full of tenderness and tears.

I breathed and they overflowed,
my heart spilled onto this pillow, silent
for I could not bear to wake you.

as the tears streamed down
and I held you, marveling,
I found my center

that place where
my will is so true
it sings in tones that weave throughout my soul.

the song of this morning
shudders through me still

utter devotion flows in balance
with the grimness of the mortal field

I have missed you for a long time
and I have no claim on you now,
nor would I wish to make one if I could

but when you wake
I will offer you these words,
my tears, my soul,
and I will rejoice for years in the memory
of the tears and the song
that found me with the light
this morning.

listen

If you would speak with me
of how to move through sadness
let me take my glasses off.

It helps me see more clearly. Not
with my eyes, not exactly. It's just
that glasses get in the way, sometimes.

They got in the way on the day
when my then-husband and I argued
loudly, about something I've forgotten.
I was sad that day. (I had
been taking care of my mother for three months then
while she struggled with cancer,
incurable, no longer in remission.)
We argued, I think, because
he didn't know I was sad.
Maybe he should have known.
Maybe I should have told him.
But such should-have-dones
have no weight for me, not now.

No, to really remember
the way my eyes can slip around my deepest needs,
to stop myself from doing that to you,
I need a more physical reminder.

You had started to tell me something
that sounded important to you.
Now, I have taken my glasses off.
I am listening with my heart
as well as my ears.
Please, continue.

narcissus

The daffodils are blooming,
and I am thinking about you.
Don't take it the wrong way; I've
always hated daffodils. Which is why
my smile was a little bitter
when I learned that the right name of the daffodil
is narcissus. That was always
something I hated about you, too.
The ability to twist everything up
until it really was all about
you. Until, no matter what I said,
somehow my thoughts were nothing more
than another proof to your point.

Well, I'm done with that now. A friend
asked, how demeaning is it to all the people
in your life, if you
think about people that way?
His incredulity freed me to say,
extremely. And it's true.

I went to the desert, where daffodils only grow
when people care to water them.
Copiously. It was easier there
to see how you were,
and to see that whether or not
you knew it, you
were pulling the water out of me
each time we spoke.

I'm back now, where water
is less rare, and
daffodils grow wild by the little stream
behind the house.

I might pick a bouquet of them for you,
give it to you next time
we meet. Killing them

would bring a deal of satisfaction
for the metaphor alone.
But I think, somehow,
that you would take the wrong point
from that gesture. I think
that the murder of the narcissus, to you,
would just be one more proof
to some point that is not mine.

I suppose I'll let the wild daffodils live.
Maybe one day, looking at them
will bring something less like hatred
more like healing. And maybe I need to remember
that the daffodils
just are
and no matter how you've twisted things up,
those little yellow bastards in the yard really
have nothing to do with you
or me. That is what
I mean.
What the narcissus mean
only they can tell.

shoulder

There is a language we share
between us, you and I.
When I lean my head
against your shoulder, I never say a word,
but I think you understand
clear as if I said it
that I know it's safe to be myself,
I know it's safe because of you.
There are no thanks that words can compass
to get this joy across
so I just lean my head against your shoulder
and I smile.
I think you feel the motion of my cheek
on your smooth shoulder, when you pull me
gently closer, kiss my hair, share a thought.
There were years when I forgot
what it was like to be this loved,
when half-measures and trying were the best
that I could see.
And now, to rest my head
on your shoulder, on our love
is more joy than I believed
the world could offer me.
When my grief comes calling and
the yellows fade to grey
there is a way I quiet down.
You came when I was quiet,
wrapped me in your arms, and said
I didn't have to worry when the shades
of sorrow called, because
your shoulders would be strong enough
to bear us both along.
Breath comes short when you say
such things as that to me,
and my heart lifts as I smile
through my tears
against your shoulder.

sing to me

On the day that I die,
when all I have been ceases
and all my gathered thoughts become
unspeakable
some words on stone will be the only way
they'd have you, stranger, believe
you could come to know me.

but a few scrawled words would not dare
scribe a circle round my life.
What could they say?
What could they possibly say?

All the things that matter
are what death takes for its own,
and death is not inclined to share.

So the only way you
could really hope
to come to know me then
would be to grind my written epitaph away,
sit on a stone you think I might have loved
and try to see the world as I once did.

Or, I suppose,
if you had the time to find such a stone,
and stay, and learn to sing
in a language stones and souls both speak,
on the day you finally devise a song that holds the space
for me
to harmonize, then, we'd have a chance to weave
a song for many worlds to hear. The harmonies
that stones can teach to those
who care to listen
is all the epitaph
I'll need.

hummingbird

it has been so long
since I believed you loved me.
really felt it, you know? held it in my gut.
maybe it was me, maybe it was you.
maybe some alchemy between us, in the air,
the place we live, the people who walk by.

maybe there is no way to make sense of how acid-sharp
and unstable we've become, in this thing we still call
love.
but I am drawn back and back again to seek some
explanation,
as a hummingbird follows the blazing trail of sweetness
to a flower. was the joy
only ever in the seeking?

I have clutched so many straws to prove you love me,
past all doubt.
but when I sit back and see my own hands reaching out,
I hate it and I hate what we've become. I know
people are not straws, to be hoarded, flourished, to
suck a living through! I *know*
I know a better way to love.

so when a hummingbird divebombed me
on the way to work last week, it
made me stop and really see. I was sure
the hummingbird was me, but now
I think it might be you.

what if I have you here, trapped in my hands,
demanding answers, demanding all I can?
if I open my hands,
drop what I've been holding
against you, back, or to my chest
could I let you fly where you will, fall
or rise, free of walls and ceilings and panes of glass and
the velvet drapes

66

we pinned up so many years ago?

why did we put those up? to keep you safe? or me?
I don't think it matters. I want to see what happens
when I tear them down, when I just let you go.

so I will set my love to ride the currents of the air
to make a trail that you, perhaps, will see
and if our love's last chance has not yet passed,
you'll be drawn to trace it, like the hummingbird, back
to me.

the offering

If I am the desert
or the desert is my soul
then you and yours
are that alchemy of light and dark and water
that makes me fertile
seeds me with tough tremulous desert plants
countless as the stars
fragile as the desert rose
improbable as living.

I can only offer you
what is, already, wholly yours.
And I can only
blaze in wonder if, offering
myself, my life, my love,
you find that we are harmony, find that we are home,
that our souls forge that exquisite ecosystem
between the outstretched pinions
of mortal hearts.

So I lay my own heart bare,
and smile, knowing you will find it no surprise.
I see you in the desert in one week.
You of many faces, many names,
you who I love, who I cannot help but love,
who I choose to love, now and always,
with all my life
and all my soul
and all my breath.

I cannot offer any less than all I am
to you. I would not be myself
if I did otherwise.

I love you
as the desert
loves the sky.

68

Precious Things

This place is full of stories. I think
that's all I'll really miss. The curtains
are down already, the rug rolled up,
the clutter of a settled life
packed away. It feels different,
what is left.

I am selling the house I grew up in.
Sitting now on a coffee table in front of the fireplace
where my mother first read to me about hobbits.
(If you only knew what that led to!)
Emptying the built-in cabinets in the dining room.
I had never seen them empty, til today.

This was my home, and in a few weeks more
I will never step within its walls again,
if all goes well. If someone else believes
they can stamp their life and memories over mine,
into these floors, these beams of rich dark wood.

For myself, I would translate the lonely walls
to walls shared, the treasures
squirreled away in every cranny
to everyday wonders to be found, picked up
by small eager hands, carried home
or given away, for friendship or for love.

That is what emptying my mother's house
has taught me.
Friendship has more value than all
the things stored up inside. I choose
to honor my friends by sharing this with them,
so it is abundance for us,
not burden for myself alone.
And I choose to honor them by leaving behind
the signifiers, the baggage, all those million things
I could let my mind turn to
instead of turning in an orbit matched to theirs.

But if I take pictures of the empty spots, outlined
in dust, where my mother's hand
arranged the potsherds, the fetishes
she'd gathered from desert and hills,
and let them sit for years untouched,
do not believe that I betray my own intent.

It's that I miss her. That is all.
Even the grey dust of her presence is as dear to me now
as the touch of her beloved hand once was.

So if I also choose these moments
of honor, and of slowness. If it takes me
a year to put her crystals out in our yard, and
if in that time I let some friendships lapse.
Understand; this is my offering
to one who loved me as much as I loved her.

I would like to do the same for everyone I love.

But I hope none of the rest of you
are planning to leave me a house so full of stories.
If you do, I think
the weight of all these precious things
would break me.

the road to ABQ

the aging biker knows
they'd find him in a ditch if he tried to ride
to Albuquerque now.

his Vietnam buddies died
from Agent Orange, he's the only one who's left
and he sounds lonely

but the stories he tells
are of family, people
supporting each other in hard times
and of the places our train slides through

the mountains will turn to pink, he says,
just around this corner.
and the wonder his voice still holds
at the birds that rise from scraggled stands of willow
makes me smile

he wants to gather sagebrush
and pile it around his living room
so the place will smell
like home. or
just smell fresh.

he laughs at the confusion
of in-law house and outhouse, and
he marvels
at the beauty of this place
just as I do, quietly,
intense.

like me, he sees the way the bushes
move, when you watch them long enough,
how they become wolves.

he used to watch the stars at night.

his words flow out like
water, like breath, like life itself,
with the easy impossible assurance
of an aging biker on his bike
down dusty desert blacktop.

there is not a ditch in sight.

the garden side of silence / sunday morning 3

There is another reality
than the one we live in now.

In that other place,
that morning,
I also woke when the light began
and the sight of you,
the feel of you
in my arms
was balm to my soul
inspiration to my words
source to my brimming tears.

but there, unlike here,
the words that welled within me
and the tears that followed them
were jewels that I kept, silent, to myself.

There,
it was not that I was afraid
but some part of me simply disbelieved
that this connection
shaking through my hands
could be more than it had already become.
Already, sleeping three times beside you,
was more than I had hoped for.
I could not imagine asking for more.

So, I woke, I wept, I was, I was, with
more clarity and truth than I could fathom ---
but in that other place
I kept my weeping as my own.

I found three sides of silence.
I did not keep my tears from myself.
I did not keep my tears silent from the world outside
myself, not quite.
But the third, I did, there. I kept my tears silent

from you.

You might have found the pillow wet
where my cheek had rested.
It wasn't likely. You might have spied
some puffiness around my eyes. But how would you
have known
what any of it meant to me?
You might have felt an echo of what moved through me
as you dreamed.
Perhaps you did, knowing you. But the choice, this time,
The choice to speak or not was mine.

No, and in that other place,
I said nothing, knowing it meant you would never know
how close to my heart you had settled already.

There is a strange and depthless beauty
in that silent place,
of words unsaid, tears still shed, potential unexplored
like a rosebud tightly curled, save for one corner of one
petal in the morning.
The feel of it thrills still within my veins.

But here, my soul,
Here there is a wildrose garden
bounded in no direction I have found.
and if the hands of this gardener
shake, sometimes --
and if the sound of your voice calling me home
still brings tears springing from my eyes -- know
that sometimes my tears resound with echoes of that
silent place that might have been
and sometimes
they simply come from being here,
with you,
here on the garden side
of silence.

III. Renewal

The Fifth Power

What is the fifth power?

This is the kind of question they would ask me
if I studied at Hogwarts, at any
magical academy. It would be a test
they gave everyone, at the end of some year
or other, a year that was hard, a year
when they might have broken, but didn't.
Mostly. And no one would remember
after taking this test, exactly
what it was that they answered,
nor would they remember, exactly
what the question was.

It would be so simple, if we could remember,
but the question flickers like dreams,
like smoke. I cough with the strength of it
when the wind is right
then it turns and I yearn
for that elusive taste to cross my tongue again.

What is the fifth power? I think
that was the question. And, what do you mean,
I want to shout at them, the invisible test-givers.
I want to shout them down in wizard-song
and prove their question is smaller than I am, less
weighty than the waiting that
has brought me to this day. No trick
question like that should be asked, not now!
This is some test, not of learning or of skill,
this is trickery, enchantment, illusion.

But I feel the question tug at me all the same. I put
my head down on the book.
I dream.

In the dream I am looking for something.
The fifth something. A power that comes

after four others. What comes in fours, and what
comes after?
Earth, air, fire, water. What's next?
Winter, spring, summer, fall, and then?
So many fours, so few fives. It must
be hidden, then, probably hidden
in plain sight, if I know aught of magic.

I race into the sky and see the world
divided in four quarters, north east south
and west dropping away below.
On I speed, past solar systems, galaxies,
the Universe itself unfolding as I pass.
Motion, then? Motion is not the fifth power,
I know this. It does not encompass.
Were there not five skandhas, I think
there were five. Yes. Matter, sensation,
perception, mental formations, consciousness?
Which of those comes last? But
those are not powers, so the final one could
not be the fifth.
All the stars go dark as these thoughts overtake me,
faster than light, and I open my eyes in blackness.
The stars have gone out. Am I
still dreaming? What kind of a question
is this, anyway? I am awake.

I am no student in a magical school.
All I could think of at first was Starhawk
and that fifth sacred thing that she
so lovingly shared, spirit. That is
not a spoiler. But spirit is also not
the fifth power.

What is it, then? Numbered, nameless,
a mere puzzle from some shaper of words?

I promise you, there is an answer.
I found it last year, a year that was hard, a year
when I might have broken, but didn't.

78

Now I claim it, or it claims me,
as I name it, so it names me.
The fifth power. The power
to renew. The power to
change, to transform. To become.

If you do not believe me, go on
with your life. A time will come
when the fifth power is all
that is left to you. Let it work within you, then.
You will change, as you must,
and you will become.

Perhaps you are the student. Perhaps
this is the test, the one test,
that will determine whether you know the world
as magic or mundane. This fifth power,
when you find it, will exalt you
or simply pass you by.
Look up when you walk. You may recognize it, or
it may recognize you.

I hope that if you see it on the road
you will call it by name
embrace it
and realize it was with you
all along.

the secret

I was terrified
when my mom got sick,
and terrified to say it, then.
I didn't know that being scared
was something I could share.
My husband, now my ex
felt too fragile, like he'd break
if I put that weight of grief and fear
on him, so I held back.

I suppose he has his own grief now,
and his own life as well.
And I have mine. I never let
that weight, that terrible dark weight
crush him. Instead, it crushed
my trust in him, it
twisted round to hurt us both.
I never saw it coming.

So, when I met you, I decided
to open up the deep place
I kept closed.
I held my heart's breath
as you looked into it,
into me, farther
than it was safe to look,
into that boundless secret keening
I keep to myself. But you
looked, and looked, and I looked back.
You held my eyes
kissed my brow, and kissed
each knuckle on my hand.

Your eyes told me
that I could be exactly
as I am.

the wind will tell you

pause -- breathe.

there is enough time to do what you need
just pause, take heed --

this is a dance, you sing all the steps
take time and remember them --
pause -- and breathe.

the sun is still moving
the monarchs are winging
all through the desert the cacti
are blooming. What you do here
is only for you. So do it as wisely
as calm and as balanced
as the ravens that watch us and laugh from the sky.
Watch them remind you --
pause -- breathe.

The dance of their wings knows nothing of rushing
nothing of haste or of human designs
They help us remember to pause, and breathe.

Pause -- take heed,
flow like the wind, smooth under their wings,
pause and remember --
flow -- breathe.

nameless

Shivers run me through.
My life is changing.

I am not in need, now. There is enough in and of me
that I can give, I can, even when it is hard, but...

where have I felt you before, you shivers coursing over
my skin?
was it when I walked alone in the high Sierra,
slept under the stars,
thought until thinking lost all meaning,
sat until I became part of the stone?

Were you with me when I saw life leave my mother's
body behind?

When I sat vigil for her, months later, in the desert she
and I both loved,
was it you -- it was, I hear you -- it was you who tuned
my inner ear
to the timbre of desert speech
and let me absorb, for a while, the deep slow-flowing
current
of the canyon
where I met my first love. It was you, it was,
you were there when the stars sang to me and the moon
went dark.
When words overbrimmed with meaning translucent as
time,
when I stepped silent off the mesa in grey light,
my vigil complete - you were there, too.

If I give you a name, shivers
if I call you intuition, if I call you -marker on the path, if
I call you beloved,
would reaching to trap you in words drive you away?

Certainly, when I look into the snow that falls to the
prairie,
when I shape these thoughts, reach forward in
this way, you wash over me unbidden.

If I had a lover like you, magical, quavering, unnamable,
they would know when to be silent, when to ask
questions,
and when to leave me curled in my cocoon of warmth,
alone,

so that in their absence I could send
this same shivering, indescribable, that I miss yet do not
miss,
back, unto the infinite spaces
where time and memory, presence and impermanence,
recognition and strangeness and wonder
dance hand in hand in shivering hand.

after the world has broken

Come to the desert.
Come with me.
There we shall burn with the stars of the firmament,
burn in the dark.

Go to the desert,
alone.
You shall walk through simplicity
stark in the light.

Be with the desert.
Be all of you.
The desert will strip away all that's untrue,
right what's askew.

And once you have been with the desert,
come home.
Home will not be the same, but
dear one, neither will you.

hold me

I have not been afraid this way before.
The fear
has nothing to do
with myself. It has everything to do
with you.

And this fear I speak of
is nothing you can fight,
not the way
you fight so many forces as you move
throughout the world.
No, the fear, this enemy
it slips beneath the floor of my awareness
spreads like a seeping black pool
and rises, slowly,
until it engulfs me in a tide of
moon-dark paralysis.

Now, love, I am afraid of the day you die.

There is little else to say.

I know no way
to battle such a fear,
founded as it is in the fabric of this place.
Even as fear trickles down my veins,
even then, part of me
still rejoices at the rooted depth of love
that wells behind and through it.

Hold me, when you are here. Please.
Let me store a lifetime of memory
against the black tide of grief
that laps patient, inexorable, at the shore
of that distant day.

The Wood

In the wood, up the hill we walk, four
strangers. I walk empty, expecting
nothing, nothing in my pockets, nothing
in my hands. the path branches to four, patterned
in brick, slanting through the trees.
we come upon an apple, broad and
fallen. It has been sliced through, dozens
of slices. Our guide offers, and
I take some, though one or two of them
have a little apple-rot on the bottom.
Would you like a few? I'm going to dry them
when I get home. On, and up
now we go, to a hillside where woven
fine blankets drape a cart by the path. No sign
tells us their story. Our guide offers again.
Another accepts, admires
the delicate patterning. And did I forget to say that the
sliced apple
was larger than my head? The slices I carry
each textbook-fat. And the blankets were woven
not by hand, but by the spiders themselves.
I have no idea how long it took them, hours,
generations. When we return
from timeless wood to the parking lot,
we are strangers no longer.
The emptiness that walked with me
like our guide is nowhere to be seen, but
the shadow of wonders hides behind my eyes.
Behind us, numberless bricked and branching paths
beckoning, the wood
grows.

People die.

Rules are made, broken. Revised or left behind.
The sun rises, sets, angles across the sky.
We laugh, we mourn, we remember, we plan.
We defy death and affirm life in every action, meaning to
or not.

Do not deny this, for you do it too.

You seek love, renown, truth, pleasure. You have no
ability or right to find them except
in proportion to how much you desire them, how much
you will sacrifice to attain them, how far
you will go to keep them. In seeking, in measuring your
desire against the world,
you find yourself.

Rain falls.

You turn within, recognize mistakes, ask the
uncomfortable questions.
You learn.
Wind cracks the trunk of the tree in the yard where you
played as a child, and it falls.

There is only so much you can do.

There is so much you can do.

Do not distract yourself with hopelessness.

Enmesh yourself in life. Do what you can. Do what you
can, with full knowledge
that you will not be here forever. Let understanding help
hone
that fine discrimination that lets you say, this is not
what I need to be doing. This is not where I

need to be. Seek out the things, the people, the places,
that fill you right up
with the certainty that this -- this time -- this is where
you need to be.
Do not settle for anything less.

Life is too short for that.
One day, you too will die.

Until that day, how will you live?
Do not answer for me. Answer for you.
No shortcuts.

Take the rest of your life by the throat, and
answer.

waking up the wild

today is slow, not lazy,
but ponderous and cool, as if time
oozed reluctantly along
all bound up with
its own concerns, nothing to do
with me

so it takes what feels like hours
to pull bag from my trash can, to
tie each shoe
remember my coat,
keys, to
respond to one more of those
everpresent emails

When at last
I walk out into darkness, bag in hand
I snuff the air, I am
a wild thing once more. I stalk
on blacktop to the dumpster.

But I recall another night
as bright as this one
when I ran the desolate trails
of a place that I know well.
I was alone. The sunlight
faded quickly. Just before it did
I saw tracks in the snow, not old,
not steaming new, but new enough
that I hefted two sharp rocks for my defense
against the cougar's spring.
I hotfooted it quick back to my car, blood
pounding, suddenly eager not for adventure,
but for warmth, electric light, a door to close
between myself and wild night.

so when the bag drops soft among its fellows, I run
arrowswift back to my door, a shadow

of that cougar on my heels. The dust
of this day's husk is gone.
the slow cool turn of time
wanders lonely in the parking lot, while inside
I build up the fire. My veins hum.

Today, cougar, and today, time,
if you cannot bear to see
how hot life's current runs in me,
turn away. I have no doubt you'll find
some other prey.

wisdom sits in places

I have heard it said
that wisdom sits in places.
I thought when I heard it
that if I sat in places, perhaps
I could become wise one day.
After an appropriate time of sitting, you understand.

But wisdom and places and time
refuse to be found when you seek them.
Then, when you relax, in some
rare moment of actual quiet,
it turns out they have been
shadowing you longer than you stalked them.

Sitting or standing, running or paused,
I do not think that I am wise
in the way I once hoped to be.
I am gentle, though, and hope is still my ally.
Perhaps, as the days flow past,
and as I see more of
hopes defeated or destroyed,
perhaps I will look back on today
and think that wisdom is
not a thing, to be gained, or lost,
but a simple way of looking at the world.

If that is so, then
I have all the permissions I need to say this.
If wisdom is a thing that you also desire,
seek it in all the ways you know.
It is within you, but it is also
without. Wisdom hides somewhere
between the world and you.
Only by knowing the world,
knowing yourself, and knowing
how little you really know
do you stand any hope of finding it.

It took death for me to understand that.

May the cost of your wisdom
be no more than you can afford
but not so small that you
underestimate the worth
of sitting in places
and letting wisdom sit beside you.

would you like to be remembered?

Who are you, when all that is not you
melts away? For what
would you like to be remembered?

Would it be your jokes, ribald or teasing,
how you always told them with
a knowing smile, like you could see
how they would make us groan,
and later how we'd laugh again together?

Or your job, all those years working hard and
thinking on your feet? I barely
know anything about it.

What about hiding the afikomen for us, telling us
in a low voice as we clustered round
that sometimes, with the smallest pieces, you could
find treasure? Where have those crackers gone,
you'd ask and we would scatter
to find where you had stashed them hours since.

Maybe you'd want to be remembered
for your love. That partnership
was beautiful, and I have seen many
in my time. The way you and Harri
moved around each other in the kitchen,
slowdancing to a tempo no one else could hear.
Well, if I loved a man like that
that love is how I'd want to be remembered.
More so if I was a man myself,
and loving him was revolution
every day.

But I asked you, and I suppose I should
give you space to answer. For what
do you want to be remembered? Or do you want
to be remembered
at all?

mind the cats

                           I have been watching cats of late.

             The way
                  they live
      is different.

The way they play, say
          what they need, what they want.

         Their utter focus on the ravens that hopped
      around the yard this morning,

                  the way they fill each stretch.

They do not strive or burn or fight
              to make the world better, but
       they do.

     I suspect cats know something about living well,
              and I, watching them,

             I have become their student.

talk me through

I've learned the hard way to take care
in matters of the heart.
That is what this is, make no mistake;
I'd know this sweet ache anywhere.
It didn't quicken in some flash from
deep within the senseless black, no, it was
the way you talk, the way you pause
to listen. The way you feel
in my hand, in my mind.
Your eyes, deep and shadowed,
tender, kind, and cruel. You said
we could talk through the night, and
we did, if talking
is sharing word and skin and soul.

I may have learned the hard way to take care,
but it's the last thing I want to do. Reality
is a poorly constructed
wall between us. How I hate it! - and how
I bare my teeth and pace its length, seek the weak spots,
find the vines.
I'd be over in a flash and in your arms,
if I could feel you waiting on the other side. But
I taste your pulse, afar, doing
what you need to do.
And I do those things too. In this now,
this kind of knowing steadies me.

But still I would unlearn this fencing, careful care. I
want to lean
against you in the desert, in a time
when such things are good to do. I hold out to you
a hand to clasp your own. Will
you grasp it, help me breach the wall?
It may be a hard way, delving deep
carving us apart to roots, uncovering foundations
we might blithely leave untouched. But what I want
why I'm asking, the simple and the true

I want you to know me
I want to know you.

Help me learn a new way to take care
in matters of the heart. Talk me
through the night again, and then let's see
what we can make of this reality.

the land of enchantment

These are the hills of enchantment
where it is not the creatures, not
the growing things,
but the bones of the land itself
that hum and buzz with magic.

Why is it that we seek
to know the names
other people have given these layers of rock?
Why do we hitch such weight to arranging things,
in time, in our own internal schemas,
rather than walking out into them
to learn how they classify themselves?
Or how they become declassified.

This is a land where crystals coalesce, where
each hidden pool of water
calls out to the sagebrush
in tones we cannot hear as we move past.
We move too quick for that, even afoot.

I know why. We want to name
these layers of rock
because we fear enchantment.
We do not want to lose our tenuous control
over living things and places.
So we cling to naming, so we strive
to classify what is unclassifiable,
classless, transcendent.

Beauty hugs the lines of these mesas,
beauty, sinuous as a snake,
follows in the heron's wake.

But if we could learn to step around
these naming systems we've built up
I think we'd find understanding there, hiding
in the land behind our shadows.

the edge

You want
to stand at the bleeding edge
of infinity. Universes
spin. You are central,
you are nothing. All that you know
has happened in the past.
Your breath forms a cloud
that resembles a camel. Your hungry eyes
create a world that lacks the meaning
you are determined to find.
Gods spring to life from the fervor
of your search. Gods die. People
also die, but that
concerns you less. You
are central. You carry reminders of how central you are
with you, always. Keychains, lists,
books, old photographs, power cords, all your life's
debris. If you let it go,
you would be nothing.
We both know that you are already
nothing. You might have been central, once,
but this is now. That was
long ago. Now: I want a new
life with you, one where
we learn how to live well,
and leave the God of so-called riches, with all
his tricks and treasures, in the dump of his designs.
You are nothing now. But knowing that,
that one thing, your eyes
need not hoard that lasting hunger you still cling to.
Set it free. Come,
stand at the bleeding edge of infinity,
stand with me.

shred your vocabulary

I need to shred your vocabulary
tear up your grand smug words
make you choke down exactly what you mean
and cough up why you mean it.

I want to set your tired thoughts alight
and watch them soar, winging with the birds;

I will have to burn your certainty to do it.

But if you have already made that leap
or better, if you
can rip the easy words from me

then I say, time to give the rest of life
a turn, relearn how to speak
and only make the promises
we keep.

M31

when the world fills up too far
I go down to sit by the water
I go down to reflect as water will
and sit until the surface stills

when every ripple vibrates to my core
and I can only miss my mother's voice
I lose the line dividing ground
from water, in my single empty eye

when the labyrinth overflows into the sky
or maybe it's the other way around
my hands can cup the nebulae, rejoice
as shining stars define my spinal cord

when the arms of this spiral galaxy cannot curve slow
    enough
to wrap around my heart
the world is not so full it cannot hold
the water and me and the endless galaxy
                                  apart.

let your eyes see

Where do we turn for guidance
when all the world is mad?
Belief wars with reason;
those we thought we could trust
tell us in every action
that they no longer walk
a path worth following.
And they have not taught us woodcraft.
They have taught us
to hold two desperate hands
over our eyes.
Only in this way can we reconcile
what we know in our hearts
with what we are told.
Only in this way
can the great deception
go on.

So take your hands away, my friends, my family.
Let your eyes see and your ears hear.
Let your heart speak. Let others listen.
Do not heed words
from the lips of those
who insist on covering their eyes
when we hold up our bleeding
hands for them to see, when we show them
with our scars
what their choices mean.

In each of you
rests the seed of power
to know the world and make it.
Take your hands from your eyes.
If we cannot find a path worth walking,
we must learn more of woodcraft, and if
even then a path does not appear
we must learn to build one,
you and I.

woman of red clay

I worked in my garden today.
Shoveled grasses, pulled up weeds,
dug the sinuous line of the channel a few feet
longer. Filled it with pebbles
against the certainty of rain.

I have sprinkled the garden with
your treasures, you know. Outside, they seem
more alive than they did
when you lived, when
you kept them trapped in bowls and boxes.

One of them caught my eye, a figure
who reminds me still of you. Tiny, clay,
red, kneeling
in prayer among the stones,
she sat on a windowsill for years
above a different garden. Today
I saw that she had changed.

She lies now on her side,
gone fetal, praying still. Time and the rain
have spared her aching knees,
and she is melting back to clay,
becoming new.

Open Your Arms

I have some things I need to say to you.
First and always, I love you.

One full year without hearing your voice hasn't changed
that.

I've lost track of how many times
you visited my dreams.
I always knew you had died. So did you.
We hugged, agreed
it was awfully nice to have this time together
without fear.

That gaping hole you left
is not closed, but its edges have become
more familiar now,
a little less jagged and raw.

I've done some things I know you'd appreciate.
I got rid of the rest of the grass in the garden.
I had help. It's all rocks now. It's beautiful.

We're adding another bench at the Sunwheel
later this year, with an inscription
in your honor. (It mentions tea, of course.)

I left someone who wasn't good for me; I found someone
who is.
I wish you could meet my beloved.

And I have a garden of my own now! I walk around it
some mornings,
scattering tobacco and cornmeal
telling all the growing things I love them.

I like to imagine I say the same things to my garden
you always said to yours,
but I will never know it, never now.

So last October I sat in darkness
for five hours on a mesa
with your ashes beside me.
I talked to you, and I talked to the desert. I listened.
When the lunar eclipse began,
I scattered you not to the wind, but around
the lone juniper that shaded you
on our last vacation.

And, of course, I miss you. I know you know it. I still
need to say it.

I miss you, and now that you are gone,
the best way for me to keep on telling you I love you
is to tell all the truest stories
of who you were.

And to drink tea. It tastes better than water.

There is one more story I have to tell,
for you, for everyone. It's hard.

It's about how one year and one day ago
we were in a hospital room.
And you were done with talking. This happened
after your last words left your lips, after you asked me
What do I have to be afraid of?

You struggled to sit up in your hospital bed.
I worried you would try to stand, try to walk, I wanted to
call a nurse,
but when you finally sat up,
all you did, all you meant to do
was open your arms
and wrap them around me.
We held each other on that terrible bed
until both my arms were numb
and you could not hold yourself up.
I know you could still hear me,

104

because your trembling eyes met mine
and you nodded when I asked
if I could help you lie down, once more
the way we did that summer.

The last choice
you made while you still breathed was
opening your arms to hold me, and
I almost stopped you. I almost
told you, save your strength, don't
sit up now. But I understood
before it was too late, and I opened
my arms to you. I let you hold me, and
I held you
for one final, endless hour.

So to you who breathe still,
I have only one thing left to say:

Open your arms to the universe.

postscript

And last, and always, and every time I make a sound:
I love you.

Acknowledgements

Like every book, this one would never have been born without support from far too many people to name.

Special thanks go out to my first Patreon supporters! Will Jennings-Hess, Eli Rubin, Clare Tessman, Megan Bowser, Donna Rubin, Cathy Dawes, Carole Anzovin, Suzi Timmermann, Carla Hinson, Miyo Davis, Jo Kenney, Zachary Ready, Tara H., Jeanine Otte, S.J. Tucker, Mykel O'Hara, Mark Barnett – your support means the world to me. Thank you for believing my voice is worth hearing.

All my readers, your feedback helped me make these poems accessible to people who weren't already inside my head. Noel Dwyer, Alex Reed, the encouragement and suggestions you offered on early and not-so-early drafts of the book were invaluable.

Most of all, Michelle Belanger, thank you for telling me that my poems were worth publishing, for being the shoulder when I needed one to cry on, for being my muse, and for asking me to marry you. Having a partner who understands and values my art, my words, and myself has made me whole again. I can offer no better thanks than saying yes, yes! With all my heart.

And thank you, reader, for walking with me awhile. To learn more about me, what I do (other than writing poems), or support my work, visit my website elyriarose.com, or find me on Patreon at patreon.com/elyria. May you find love in our world deep enough to help heal your sorrows. And if this book has helped you, please share it with others who have lost loved ones, who could use a little quiet empathy and understanding, whenever they are ready.

love,
Elyria

Made in the USA
Lexington, KY
02 June 2017